MINIBEAST ADVENTURE

EMILY KINGTON

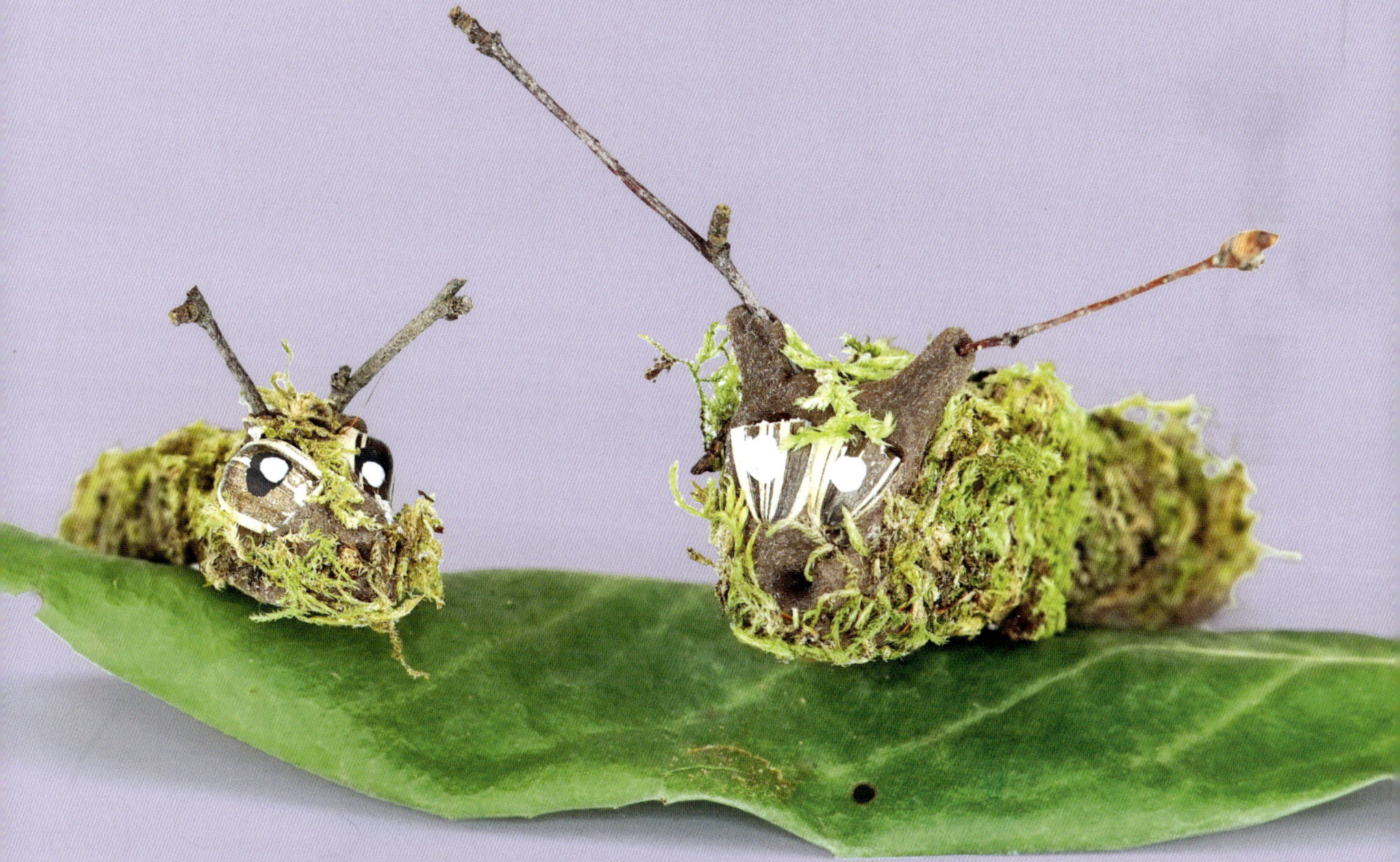

CONTENTS

It's brilliant getting outside, discovering things together, whatever the time of year. This book is all about understanding, looking after, finding and making all things minibeast. It's fun, it's interesting and it's smart!

Get your wellies on and take a close look at what is out and about. Learn how to become a bug detective, make a home for bugs, attract different species, and lots more...

NATURE HUNT CHALLENGE — 4

LET'S GO ON A BUG HUNT! — 6

BUG HOTEL — 10

ANIMAL WALKING STICKS — 12

MAKE YOUR OWN SPIDER — 14

MAKE YOUR OWN CATERPILLAR — 15

NEED HELP?
Watch out for this sign throughout the book. You may need help from an adult when completing these tasks.

MORE BUG FRIENDS 16

BUG CITY 18

BE A BUG DETECTIVE 22

TAKE CARE OUT AND ABOUT 24

NATURE HUNT CHALLENGE

For some of these projects, you will need to take time out and go on a nature hunt!

NATURE HUNT SAFETY

Never go out into nature alone; make sure to always go with an adult and stay together to keep safe. It can be easy to get distracted but be careful not to get separated.

Beware, some bugs can be poisonous and may bite.

Always wash your hands after handling bugs or soil.

TAKING CARE OF THE ENVIRONMENT

Only collect nature finds from the ground. Don't pick anything off trees or plants like branches or leaves as that will damage the plant.

Treat insects with care and don't forget to release them.

STONES AND PEBBLES

Look for all kinds of stones, including those of different shapes, sizes and colours.

LEAVES

Search for leaves on fallen branches and the ground. The more different shapes and sizes the better.

STICKS

You want to find lots of different size sticks for crafting with.

MOSS

Find moss growing in woods, on fallen branches or on the forest floor. Only take a little from an area where there is already a lot.

ALL SORTS

Pine cones, acorns and seeds.

VINES

Vine stems are good for holding things together because they're so strong.

MUD, MARVELLOUS MUD!

Lovely sticky mud – the stickier the better. An alternative would be to use paper clay.

WOOD AND BARK

Look for interesting pieces of wood and loose bark.

DRY GRASS OR STRAW

Minibeasts love these materials – search the ground to collect it up.

YOU WILL ALSO NEED:

- Gloves
- Wellington boots
- Old bag (to carry items home)
- Small trowel/old spoon (for collecting mud)
- Strong glue
- PVA glue
- Sandpaper
- Acrylic paints
- Paintbrushes
- Small wooden box
- Magnifying glass
- Small trowel
- Small old container
- Water

LET'S GO ON A BUG HUNT!

Make a list of the top 10 bugs that you would like to find. Put a tick against them when you find them. Here's 10 of our top favourite bugs.

BUG SAFETY

- You must take care if you live in a place where there are biting or poisonous bugs and animals.

- Ask an adult to help you, in case there is something dangerous lurking under dead leaves or logs.

- Always put insects back after you finish observing them in their habitat.

- Always wear gloves on a bug hunt.

TOOLS

- Take a magnifying glass to help you spot and study tiny insects.

- Take your own notepad to write down all the bugs you find!

GARDEN SNAILS

As a snail grows, their shell grows too. Snails mainly come out at night time, but if you peek under leaves on trees and plants, you might find them snoozing there, because that is what they like to eat!

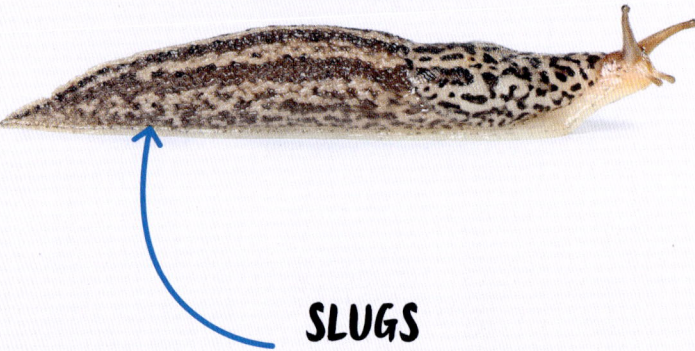

SLUGS

Slugs leave a slime trail so they are easy to track! The slime protects their tummies from the rough ground. The best time to find them is in the early morning dew.

BEETLES
Most beetles can fly, but they spend most of their time on the ground. Most only live for a year, but there are hundreds of thousands of different kinds. Search under dry leaves, you will find them there!

MILLIPEDES
Millipedes have hard outer shells which they shed as they grow. They like to live in dark, damp places because this is where they can find rotting leaves to eat.

BLACK ANTS
Ants can be found everywhere on Earth. They can lift 10 to 50 times their body weight! See if you can spot them doing just that!

SPIDERS

Look for webs! Spiders usually aren't far away. There are lots of different kinds of spiders and they mostly eat insects. Not all spiders spin webs but when they do it is to trap insects to eat.

WOODLICE

Woodlice have 14 legs and an outer shell. They especially like dark, damp places. Look for them under rotting wood, you are likely to find lots of them there!

EARTHWORMS

Worms need moisture, so they live in moist soil underground. They come out at night to eat leaves and in the daytime when it's raining!

STICK INSECTS

Stick insects are clumsy fliers and usually fly only in short bursts. They are, though, very good at not moving for long periods of time to avoid being spotted by prey. Good luck finding one - they do look just like sticks!

LADYBIRDS

Farmers like ladybirds because they have BIG appetites, they eat bugs that are plant-eating pests. They are out and about, almost anywhere, from March through to October.

HOW DID YOU GET ON? 10 OUT OF 10 IF YOU FOUND ANY STICK INSECTS - THEY ARE MASTERS OF DISGUISE!

BUG HOTEL

You can make an excellent home for very tiny insects. It's like a natural jigsaw puzzle and is perfect for important mini-bugs.

> **YOU WILL NEED:**
> - Thin and chunky sticks
> - Dry grass or straw
> - Moss
> - Dry bark
> - Pebbles or stones
> - Acorn tops
> - Conkers (or any other seeds)
> - Pine cones
> - Small wooden box

1. Find a small wooden box.

2. Start with a layer of chunky sticks on one side and thin sticks on the other.

3. Build the next layer with lots of moss on one side, bark on the other and some dry grass or straw on top.

4. Finish with a layer of pebbles, acorn tops, pine cones and conkers, or any other seeds you can find.

PLACE IN A QUIET SPOT IN YOUR GARDEN OR BALCONY AND MAKE A DIARY FOR RECORDING WHO CHECKS IN!

ANIMAL WALKING STICKS

It's always handy to have a walking stick on a nature hunt. You can use it to poke around in hidden places and see what you can find!

YOU WILL NEED:
- A strong stick that comes up to your waist!
- Sandpaper
- PVA glue
- Acrylic paint
- Paintbrushes

1. Take time to find the right stick. One that has a natural handle at one end, like this, is perfect.

You may need an adult to cut it to the right size for you.

2. Clean the stick and remove any flaking bark. Use sandpaper to get the surface smooth and ready to paint.

3. Paint a bright and fun animal design onto your walking stick and leave it to dry. Then, give the walking stick two coats of PVA glue. Let it dry between coats.

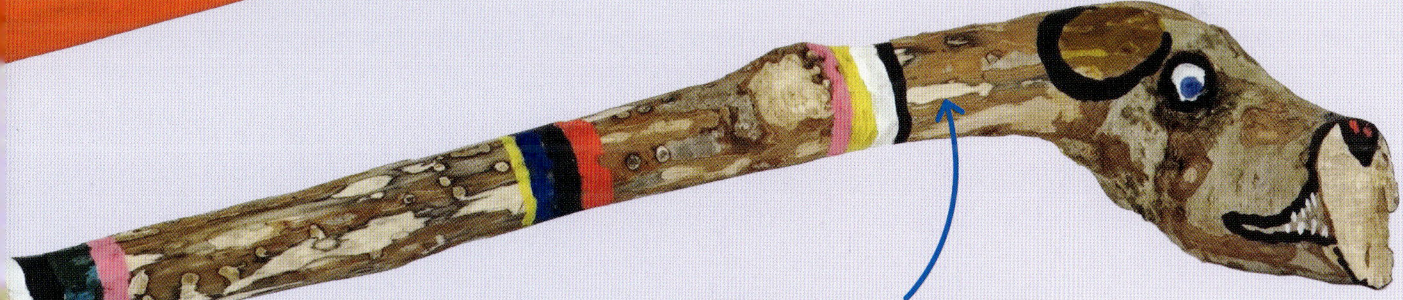

The glue will protect the stick's painted surface.

YOUR HUNTS WILL BE A BREEZE FROM NOW ON: USE YOUR STICK TO MOVE STONES AND LEAVES TO FIND HIDDEN TREASURES!

MAKE YOUR OWN SPIDER

Make some larger-than-life bugs with your nature hunt finds! Try making a creepy spider!

YOU WILL NEED:
- Sticky mud or glue
- A round stone
- Pebbles and tiny stones
- A small piece of bark
- 8 leaf stems or small twigs

Spiders have eight legs.

1. Find a round stone to use as the spider's body. Use sticky mud or glue to attach tiny stones for eyes.

2. Put a sticky blob of mud onto the piece of bark. Push eight leaf stems or small twigs into the mud.

3. Add a little more sticky mud and push the head into place in the middle of the bark.

Make lots of spiders using different coloured stones.

MAKE YOUR OWN CATERPILLAR

Try making this awesome, hairy caterpillar. Display it on a leaf to make it look more life-like!

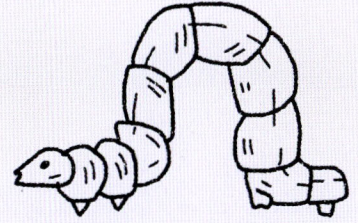

YOU WILL NEED:
- Small sticks
- Sticky mud
- Glue
- Moss
- Seeds
- A big leaf

1. Select sticks that are different lengths, so that you can make one small and one larger caterpillar.

2. Wrap the sticks in sticky mud.

Leaf stems make great antennae.

3. Before the mud dries, cover it in moss. Add some seeds for the eyes, using glue to hold them in place.

4. Make your caterpillar a friend. Arrange them on a big leaf, as this is what a caterpillar would eat!

DID YOU KNOW?

Once fully grown, a caterpillar forms itself into a pupa (or chrysalis), a kind of cocoon. It does this once it's ready to change into a butterfly or moth. A caterpillar is also able to spin a kind of sticky silk, attaching itself to a branch or leaf whilst it transforms.

MAKE MORE BUG FRIENDS FOR YOUR SPIDER AND CATERPILLARS! GET CREATIVE WITH YOUR NATURE FINDS BY MAKING FLYING BUGS.

Shiny leaves suit this flying insect.

A stick makes the perfect body.

Adding vine antennae can make your bugs look even more real!

Small, colourful leaves look like the wings of a moth or butterfly! How many different leaves can you find to use?

This bug has just landed on a dry piece of bark.

BUG CITY

Here are some ideas for creating a whole city for bugs of all kinds, shapes and sizes. Keep an eye on your city to see who moves in!

YOU WILL NEED:

- Fallen branches
- Sticks and branches
- Rotten wood
- Moss
- Pebbles and small stones
- Flat stones for the track
- Leaves
- Bark
- Dry grass or straw
- A small trowel for digging
- A small old container for the pond
- Water

TOP TIP

Get creative! Any nature find can be used to create your bug city if you put your imagination to it. These are just a few ideas to get you started.

SHELTER

All cities need shelter! These are safe places where bugs can hide.

Create a dry place for bugs to stay - a stick camp with a dry grass floor is ideal.

You can dig a small cave into the side of a bank or hill to make a safe, dark shelter.

WATER

Just like humans, bugs need plenty of water and food to live.

Some bugs like to be near water, so dig a hole big enough to fit a small container all the way up to its rim. Fill it with water and surround it with small pebbles and stones.

HIDING PLACES

Bugs can be shy creatures! Give them plenty of hiding places in your bug city.

Scrape out a shallow track and lay down flat stones - there will be bugs that want to live underneath.

Make a leaf pile for all of the bugs that like to hide in them. Sweep a pile together from your garden!

SHADE

Help the bugs stay cool by making lots of shady places for them to go to.

Just like us, bugs need to keep cool. A row of sticks standing up in the soil can provide can provide some much needed shade on a hot day.

Or make a pile of sticks and bark to create a cool home for tiny bugs.

A small pile of sticks is a cool home for tiny bugs.

You might see a woodlouse in your bug city if you stack pieces of bark.

THE BUG CITY

Good luck building your bug city - enjoy watching its visitors all year long.

Green leaves can be a very tasty treat. For bugs who like damp spaces, include some rotten wood covered in moss.

Build the bug city walls with fallen branches - they will attract insects, too.

In spring and summer, add some flowers to attract bees searching for pollen.

KEEP A RECORD THROUGH THE CHANGES IN SEASONS, STUDY THE BUGS, AND KEEP ADDING INTERESTING NATURE HUNT FINDS.

BE A BUG DETECTIVE

We may not always see bugs, but what they leave behind tells us they were there. Here are some interesting things to look out for.

Damaged leaves from hungry caterpillars.

CATERPILLAR FOOD

Lots of insects eat leaves, but this caterpillar has been caught red-handed!

Bees and wasps can sting if they feel threatened - so don't bother the nest.

BEE AND WASP NESTS

Bees and wasps aren't too fussy where they build nests. Some decide on a natural location, such as a hollow tree, but often you will see them on buildings. Some even nest underground! Being dry and safe is a priority.

WORM CASTINGS

These are small mounds or bumps on the surface of a lawn which are basically worm poo! Don't worry: it's really good for the grass as it's highly nutritious poo!

ROUGH WOOD

Wasps often chew the surface of wooden posts and garden furniture. Run your hand over the surface and it will have a rough feel. Wasps mix strips of wood with saliva to make part of their nests.

SLUG AND SNAIL TRAILS

Slugs and snails often leave a silvery track of mucus on surfaces as they slide along. The mucus also helps them stick to things, which is especially useful when climbing.

ANT HILLS

Armies of worker ants carry small bits of earth, grit or sand to the surface. If you see one of these hills, you know that lots of ants are living underground.

SPIDER WEBS

Some spiders spin webs to catch prey. It's an ingenious way to catch your dinner without having to chase it down!

TAKE CARE OUT AND ABOUT

It's always brilliant fun when you are out exploring and gathering, but it's a good idea to take some things with you to stay safe.

WATER
Take plenty of water. It's easy to become dehydrated in active play.

FIRST AID KIT
Take along a basic first aid kit to deal with scratches and insect bites.

CLOTHING
Wear appropriate clothing and footwear. It can be slippery and wet in woody areas.

SAFETY FIRST

- Never eat any part of a plant or fungus or drink water from a stream.
- Climbing is fun and a real achievement, but check with adults before climbing anything and make sure they stay around to help you. It's not safe to climb alone.
- Beware of dangerous or poisonous wild plants and animals (applicable in some areas).
- Be careful near water. It can often be deeper than it looks.

ALWAYS ASK AN ADULT BEFORE YOU DO ANY OF THE PROJECTS IN THIS BOOK!

Copyright © 2024 Hungry Tomato Ltd

First published in 2024 by Hungry Tomato Ltd
F15, Old Bakery Studios, Blewetts Wharf, Malpas Road, Truro, Cornwall, TR1 1QH, UK.

No part of this publication may be reproduced, stored in a retrieval system, or transmitted in any form or by any means, electronic, mechanical, photocopying, recording, or otherwise, without prior written permission of the copyright owner.

A CIP catalogue record for this book is available from the British Library.

ISBN 9781835693568

Printed in China

Discover more at
www.hungrytomato.com

Picture credits:
Abbreviations: m-middle, t-top, l-left, r-right, bg-background.

Shutterstock: Alex Staroseltsev 9br; Boliglov Andrew 19br; Chris Moody 8b; cynoclub 9t; Encierro 24tm; Eric Isselee 7m, 7bl; guy42 6b; Hanahstocks 2bm; Hchjjl 12tr, 14tr, 15tr, (warning sign used throughout); Henrik Larsson 8m; Ian Grainger 23br; ILYA AKINSHIN 23mr; Klingsup 2tm; Monkey Business Images 24tr; Oakland Images 24tl; padung 3b, 22tl; pp 8b; r.classen 6tr; schankz 22tr; SJ Travel Photo and video 2br; SKphotographer 8t; Svetlana Lukienko 3bl; Thijs de graaf 23tl; Torychemistry 23br.

Every effort has been made to trace the copyright holders, and we apologise in advance for any unintentional omissions. We would be pleased to insert the appropriate acknowledgements in any subsequent edition of this publication.